ENDORSEMENT

Sherita White has written a compelling book about the long-lasting impact that words can have on your personal and spiritual life. Ms. White compassionately addresses the sensitive subject matter of verbal abuse, and equips the reader with powerful tools based on the Word of God to overcome the schemes of the enemy who seeks to kill, steal, and destroy. Upon reading this timely and relevant book, you will be renewed in the spirit of your mind and empowered to do all things through Christ Who strengthens you!

Andrea J. Dixon-Seahorn, Ed. D, Author of
*She Wears It Well: Essential Qualities
of the Women God Designed You to Be*

BROKEN BY MAN'S WORDS
HEALED BY GOD'S WORDS

SHERITA C. WHITE

EDITED BY
NICOLE QUEEN

VISION PUBLISHING
HOUSE

Vision Publishing House
www.vision-publishinghouse.com

ISBN: 978-1-955297-26-4 (Paperback)

This book is dedicated to my daughter, Promise Anthonia White. Remember who you are and remember who you belong to. You belong to the Lord Jesus Christ. Know your worth, and remember you are who God says you are. May God's voice and The Word of God (Bible) speak louder than any other voice on the earth! Remember, "For thou hast possessed my reins: thou hast covered me in my mother's womb. I will praise thee; for I am fearfully and wonderfully made: marvellous are thy works; and that my soul knoweth right well" (Psalm 139:13-14 KJV). Mommy loves you very much. You are totally awesome with your long legs!

The Word of God is the heartbeat of God, and His Word is alive because His breath was the Word of God.

— HEBREWS 4:12, PARAPHRASED

CONTENTS

THE IMPORTANCE OF WORDS

*"The tongue has the power of life and death, and
those who love it will eat its fruit."*

— PROVERBS 18:21 KJV

Consider the old saying we used to hear growing up: "Sticks and stones may break your bones, but words will never hurt you." While this sounds good, this statement is the furthest from the truth. There is no denying that words have the power to hurt you, and if an individual repeatedly uses negative words, it can have a long-lasting effect on you. Words can be used in a hurtful way to attack someone's character or to undermine their well-being. Destructive words can also lead to emotional trauma.

Words can lift you up or cast you down; that's how powerful words are! Therefore, we ought to take great care when we speak (James 1:19). The tongue, though a minor member of the body, can serve two purposes: to speak blessings or curses.

"Out of the same mouth come praise and cursing.
My brothers and sisters, this should not be."

— JAMES 3:10 KJV

Depending on how words are used, they can cause harm, harass, scold, label, disarm, victimize, destroy, or control you. Or, words can be used to encourage, strengthen, revive, uplift, or lovingly correct you.

Oftentimes, those who are closest to us can damage us the most. I have experienced this in my own life. There was a time when I strongly disagreed with one individual in particular. There was a lot of back and forth when the disagreement started to escalate. Then, things took a turn for the worse. It went from arguing to name-calling, insults, and disrespect, which took it to another level. After that, the individual began discussing what other individuals had said about me. It did not bother me initially because I knew most of it was untrue. However, I was determined not to allow this person to continue to talk negatively about me because I knew what God said about me. We can reject negative conversations and words when we know what God says about us.

Eventually, the other person said something that changed the entire atmosphere. It pierced my soul like a sharp knife, and something inside me broke. I felt like I had lost my will to defend myself or fight back with words. I was rendered power-less by the words of this person. My eyes began to well up with tears as I grew quieter. After those words, all I could do was cry out to God. I was so hurt that words could make me feel that way. As a result of that encounter, I have learned to walk away from disagreements when people raise their voices or are being disrespectful. Before things get out of hand, walking away and praying is best.

Someone once told me that it's not a big deal and that words don't really matter. In some cases, it may not be a big deal, but words do matter in the larger scheme of things. Do you know that ill words can physically make a person sick? It can cause headaches and different illnesses. So, removing yourself from that kind of environment may be necessary.

The Word of God says, "Thou art snared with the words of thy mouth, thou art taken with the words of thy mouth" (Proverbs 6:2 KJV). The enemy uses words to harm and trap us, but God's Word always prevails. We must be aware that God's word cancels out any assignment of the enemy; we must also be careful not to speak from our flesh.

A great woman of God, Cindy Trimm, publicly shared her testimony. She talked about the power of words in her testimony. In her youth, she made a vow that she would die around 40. As a young girl, she considered 40 years old to be old. Consequently, when she reached the age of 39, she began to experience illnesses. After that, the Lord reminded her of a vow she made as a child. Because Cindy's words brought physical affliction to herself, she had to renounce that vow to continue to live and fulfill God's plan for her life.

Our lives can still be affected by spoken words, even if we don't believe them, due to our limited understanding. Therefore, we must recite God's words and confess such things as:

I am a royal priesthood.
I am a Child of God.
I am an overcomer.

Words can be used as a weapon in the natural and spiritual realm, according to 2 Corinthians 10:4-6. God's Word in Revelation states, "Coming out of his mouth is a sharp sword with which to strike down the nations. 'He will rule them with an iron scepter.' He treads the winepress of the fury of the wrath of God Almighty" (Revelation 19:15 NIV). It is astonishing to think that the Lord's Word is like a sharp sword (Hebrews 4:12). In the same way He has authority with His words, He also allows us to have authority.

The world was created by God, whether you believe in Him or not. John 1:1 states, "In the beginning was the Word, and the Word was with God, and the Word was God." God is the originator and the best Language Arts teacher in the universe. The world was created and manifested through words. As a result, we can now see how important and powerful words are.

The words you use can create the world you live in. God created the earth with His word; because of this, we should be careful not to say things out of anger. Thankfully, God allows us grace and enables us to speak His truth to cancel out what we may have said (Isaiah 30:18).

Have you ever regretted something you've said? I'm sure many of us have. My spiritual father in the Gospel, Bishop Daniel M. Jordan, told me that every experience is not a wasted experience.

> *"And he said unto me, My grace is sufficient for thee: for my strength is made perfect in weakness. Most gladly therefore will I rather glory in my infirmities, that the power of Christ may rest upon me."*
>
> — 2 CORINTHIANS 12:9 KJV

WORDS! WORDS! WORDS!

Throughout our lives, words are interwoven into our daily routines. Every day, we must decide how to use our words. We should use words kindly and respectfully (Ephesians 4:32). God's grace gives us a choice and teaches us how to interact with one another.

What if we took the time to think before we spoke? Could we avoid hurt and misunderstandings? Sometimes, we may judge others based on what someone has said about them.

> *"Judge not, that ye be not judged. For with what judgment ye judge, ye shall be judged: and with what measure ye mete, it shall be measured to you again."*
>
> — MATTHEW 7:1-2 KJV

A wise woman once told me that the best way to form an opinion about someone is to get to know them for yourself. Perception plays an important role. One person's perception of something can offend another, but another person's perception could mean something completely different. That's why it's crucial to gain a deeper understanding. The Word of God states, "Wisdom is the principal thing; therefore get wisdom: and with all thy getting get understanding" (Proverbs 4:7 KJV).

There are times when people have held onto grudges for years based on what someone has told them that may not have been true. The Bible states, "A brother offended is harder to be won than a strong city: and their contentions are like the bars of a castle" (Proverbs 18:19 KJV). In a way, it's like a prison for both of them; one may be trying to escape, while the other keeps them captive. Once there has been an apology, we must take a conscious decision to stand up and shake the dust off our feet (Matthew 10:4). This is what God's Word instructs us to do. We must go and correct our mistakes. Since the Lord has shown us grace and mercy, we must show mercy to others.

> *"If a man say, I love God, and hateth his brother, he*
> *is a liar: for he that loveth not his brother whom*
> *he hath seen, how can he love God whom he*
> *hath not seen?"*

> — 1 JOHN 4:20 KJV

One thing to consider is that it is possible to have an unhealthy relationship with the Lord, especially if it is performance-based instead of grace-based. When we are offended by His creation and filled with bitterness and strife, it is difficult to communicate with Him. It should be our desire to ask the Lord for the ability to forgive as quickly as He does.

Feelings of unforgiveness and grudges are binding. It is a horrible feeling, like carrying a heavy burden with you all the time. It is understandable why God hates unforgiveness.

> *But if ye forgive not men their trespasses, neither*
> *will your Father forgive your trespasses.*

> — MATTHEW 6:15 KJV

No one has a right to hold things against someone else when God has forgiven us of many things. Therefore, my constant prayer is that the Lord forgives me and helps me forgive others. Forgiveness is freedom! I have learned that forgiveness doesn't necessarily mean reconciliation. Sometimes it is best to forgive, adapt, and move forward because we can't force another person to change their behaviors. Only God can do this!

There is a strong connection between feelings and words. We can use words to express love or hatred. God gave us words as a gift. The Lord wants us to live peacefully with all men (Romans 12:18).

> *"Let your speech be always with grace, seasoned with salt, that ye may know how ye ought to answer every man."*
>
> — COLOSSIANS 4:6 KJV

Some refuse to be at peace, which is when the enemy uses words to do the opposite of what God intends. Words were created by God to uplift, encourage, and create life. The enemy perverts God's words. The enemy's goal is to break us by using word curses. The enemy uses words in music, movies, and social media in the entertainment industry. Scripture further confirms this truth.

> *"Be sober, be vigilant; because your adversary the devil, as a roaring lion, walketh about, seeking whom he may devour."*
>
> — 1 PETER 5:8 KJV

Despite the enemy's desire to use words to bring death, God uses words to bring life. This is why we must be careful and not allow the enemy's words to affect us; we must counteract his words with God's Words.

The most dangerous person in the world can be someone we confide in and share our secrets with, or even someone we seek forgiveness from. Have you ever asked for forgiveness and confessed your wrongdoing to someone? When you addressed this person, did they claim to have sincerely forgiven you, but later used it against you? Consequently, this may put you in a vulnerable position. However, God will see your effort and restore you even if the other person doesn't do their part. I am grateful that Lord doesn't hold our past against us. In his teaching, Bishop Daniel M. Jordan once said, "He was hung up for our hang up." This means that all of our past mistakes were hung on the Cross with Jesus when He died for us; He no longer holds the former things against us.

> *"Remember ye not the former things, neither consider the things of old. Behold, I will do a new thing; now it shall spring forth; shall ye not know it?"*
>
> — ISAIAH 43:18-19A KJV

The Lord gives us instructions for handling these situations when someone reveals their secrets and sins.

> *"He that covereth a transgression seeketh love; but he that repeateth a matter separateth very friends."*
>
> — PROVERBS 17:9 KJV

> *"Brethren, if a man be overtaken in a fault, ye which are spiritual, restore such an one in the spirit of meekness; considering thyself, lest thou also be tempted."*
>
> — GALATIANS 6:1 KJV

EFFECTIVE COMMUNICATION

Communication is vital to any successful relationship; it works two ways. You must listen to communicate effectively. When we listen to someone, we acknowledge their importance. Have you ever spoken to someone and they were distracted? Was their attention divided? Was the conversation completely one-sided? This may have made you feel that what you're saying wasn't necessary or important.

Our Heavenly Father manages the entire universe, but He always has time to listen to us and hear our needs. He bends down to give us the attention we need.

> *"Because he hath inclined his ear unto me, therefore will I call upon him as long as I live."*
>
> — PSALM 116:2 KJV

Even when we are rushing through our day, He is still patient and available. He always makes you feel like you're the only person in the whole wide world. Imagine talking to the Lord, and He was too busy to listen. It could be an emergency situation for you, but what if He said, "Hold on, I'm busy taking care of something else?" However, He's not like that. He is such a gentleman and always gives us His undivided attention.

Our challenge is to stop and listen to others, as our Heavenly Father does for us. However, if we can't listen to them at that time, we should try to set a time when we can. Likewise, we should set a time to meet with Our Father. This is how we can let Him know that He is our priority. Then, after we finish talking to the Father, we should listen and allow Him to speak. Listening restores and renews our faith (Romans 10:17). We should pray and ask Holy Spirit to help us to listen more than we speak.

> *"Wherefore, my beloved brethren, let every man be*
> *swift to hear, slow to speak, slow to wrath."*
>
> — JAMES 1:19 KJV

There may be times when you are speaking with your friends and talking over each other due to excitement. However, you must be careful to let each other speak, or else you may not be able to hear one another. In other situations, you may be frustrated with someone and jump to a conclusion. It's important to always give that other person an opportunity to speak so that you can hear the whole story.

> *"Let us hear the conclusion of the whole matter:*
> *Fear God, and keep his commandments: for this*
> *is the whole duty of man."*
>
> — ECCLESIASTES 12:13 KJV

When you interrupt someone while they are speaking, it can be perceived as rudeness. That's why it's essential to listen. Therefore, we should pray and ask the Holy Spirit to help us communicate effectively to have healthy and whole relationships.

PERSONAL REFLECTION

The Bible says that life and death are in the power of the tongue (Proverbs 18:21). Today, I challenge you to be more intentional about speaking to others. How can you use your words to bring life to yourself and others?

_____

_____

_____

_____

_____

_____

_____

_____

_____

_____

_____

_____

_____

_____

_____

_____

_____

_____

_____

_____

_____

_____

_____

_____

_____

_____

TYPES OF WORDS

*"A soft answer turneth away wrath: but grievous
words stir up anger. The tongue of the wise
useth knowledge aright: but the mouth of fools
poureth out foolishness. The eyes of the Lord are
in every place, beholding the evil and the good.
A wholesome tongue is a tree of life: but
perverseness therein is a breach in the spirit. A
fool despiseth his father's instruction: but he
that regardeth reproof is prudent."*

— PROVERBS 15:1-5 KJV

Words can significantly impact our lives,
depending on the types of words and how they're
used. Words can cause joy or sadness, and cause
others to flourish or diminish. We were taught a plethora of
words in school, and how they are used to communicate effectively. Some types are: adjectives, verbs, nouns, pronouns,

prepositions, and conjunctions. Words make up a sentence; sentences make up paragraphs. Every word matters!

SPOKEN WORDS

Words can be used to compliment or criticize, which can impact our daily lives. For this reason, we should begin speaking life early over our children, spouses, and the Body of Christ. The words we speak over our children can carry them throughout their entire lives. For instance, a parent telling their child that they can do it, that they're smart, and that they're pretty/ handsome will positively affect their lives. However, there can be a negative effect on them when they hear words from their parent, such as: "You're stupid. You're ugly. You can't do anything right." We should teach our children to speak kindly to themselves and others. How we speak to one another can make our relationships healthy or unhealthy.

God is so awesome and understands the impact of words. Therefore, He left His Holy Word with us on Earth. There are times to be quiet and speak (Ecclesiastes 3:7). We have to speak The Word of God out loud because speaking is key to causing things to move in the atmosphere (Mark 11:22-24). The Lord wants us to move our mountains by speaking to them. We must speak His Word for healing. We must speak His Word over our hearts, children, spouses, friendships, relationships, circumstances, minds, and situations. It's easy to speak to the Lord with your thoughts, but we must speak them out loud. The Lord wants us to be victorious and not a victim. Therefore, we must speak the Word!

God's Word stands forever; it's long-lasting, permanent, and never stops. That's why the enemy fights us Believers who read and believe in the Word of God because it will literally change and rearrange our lives with faith. The Word of God is powerful and creative! The Bible contains words that allow us to see how words are used. Words are creative and can manifest things. Words spoken by God created our lives and our world. The Bible is a prophetic voice that spoke the earth into existence. It will continue to be prophetic because it reveals Our Creator. Let's examine the words in Genesis that God spoke to create the world.

> *"In the beginning God created the heaven and the earth. And the earth was without form, and void; and darkness was upon the face of the deep. And the Spirit of God moved upon the face of the waters. And God said, Let there be light: and there was light. And God saw the light, that it was good: and God divided the light from the darkness. And God called the light Day, and the darkness he called Night. And the evening and the morning were the first day. And God said, Let there be a firmament in the midst of the waters, and let it divide the waters from the waters.*

> — GENESIS 1:1-6 KJV

Although we know the importance of God's Word, some may often forget its effects. There's a famous saying: "If you cannot say anything nice, do not say anything at all." This is because words can affect us positively and negatively once spoken.

We find in the Bible that the Word was God, Himself, speaking to us.

"In the beginning was the Word, and the Word was with God, and the Word was God."

— JOHN 1:1 KJV

Later in the chapter, it states:

"And the Word was made flesh, and dwelt among us (and we beheld his glory, the glory as of the only begotten of the Father) full of grace and truth."

— JOHN 1:14 KJV

God created time. In time, all things are manifested in our life, good or bad. His ways are not our ways, and His thoughts are not our thoughts. God knows the words we will speak before we even speak.

The Lord is very concerned about us as His Children; therefore, we should watch what we say. He takes what we say so seriously that it is recorded in heaven, where we will have to give an account. Thus, we have to repent daily for our actions and thoughts.

Many of us have been taught not to question the Lord, but to receive an answer from the One who knows all, you must ask of Him (James 4:2b). Scripture declares that we have not because we ask not. So, one day, I asked the Lord several questions.

I asked the Lord, "Why are words so important? Why not use another method of communication? We can communicate with our eyes and use our hands for sign language. But why words?" He allowed me to understand that words can change and create environments.

Then, I asked the Lord, "How is it that the beginning was the Word? How was the Word with God and God, all at the same time?" The Lord responded to my inquiries. He said, "The Word was inside of Me. So when I spoke, it revealed my heart." This means that God released what was already in Him. So, it also means that what's in you and me will manifest outwardly. That's why we must study God's Word and hide His Word in our hearts.

> *"Thy word have I hid in mine heart, that I might not sin against thee."*
>
> — PSALM 119:11 KJV

Also, when we study the Word of God, the Holy Spirit will remind us of what's in us.

> *"But the Comforter, which is the Holy Ghost, whom the Father will send in my name, he shall teach you all things, and bring all things to your remembrance, whatsoever I have said unto you."*
>
> — JOHN 14: 26 KJV

> *"If ye abide in me, and my words abide in you, ye shall ask what ye will, and it shall be done unto you."*
>
> — JOHN 15:7 KJV

The Word was manifested in the flesh. In other words, the Word came alive. When we understand the power of words, we may not want to speak so quickly, because words are influential. Has the Holy Spirit ever encouraged you not to say something? But in anger, you have you spew it out? And afterward, did you feel a change in the atmosphere— shifting from good, to bad, to ugly? But Holy Spirit told you to hold your peace. However, sometimes we feel like we have to have the last word.

We have to be careful about what we say about ourselves. The Lord's intention was for people to build each other up with kind words, but the enemy will always do the opposite. The devil comes to kill, steal and destroy, while God comes to give us life abundantly. God uses His Word to build, correct, and instruct.

> *"All scripture is given by inspiration of God, and is profitable for doctrine, for reproof, for correction, for instruction in righteousness."*
>
> — 2 TIMOTHY 3:16 KJV

A person may say, "It's just words." But in reality, it's more than just words; they have meaning and are very impactful. The Bible wouldn't be necessary or meaningful, if it was just a random book of words strung together. We receive guidance and direction from the Bible.

Words have significant meaning. They can transform, deliver, encourage, and give hope. You may have heard the saying: "Take Him at His Word." This means to take what the Lord has spoken and apply it to your life and circumstances. Believe it and trust it.

Because Isaiah 53:5 KJV says, "With His stripes we are

healed," then we are healed. The Bible also says, "Trust in the Lord with all thine heart; and lean not unto thine own understanding. In all thy ways acknowledge Him, and He shall direct thy paths" (Proverbs 3:5-6 KJV). Therefore, we must trust in the Lord and be confident regarding how He leads us.

The Bible was not written merely for the sake of writing; it was established to produce results. However, the enemy wants us to forget that; he wants us to be quiet and forsake the power of the spoken word. If we ever begin to speak God's Word boldly, we will see things change.

I learned a tough lesson from my spiritual father in the Gospel. He taught us to tell God our sorrows and tell people our joys, but often, we do the opposite. We confide in people with our sorrows, which is not always beneficial, especially if you do not want what was shared to be repeated.

> *"A talebearer revealeth secrets: but he that is of a*
> *faithful spirit concealeth the matter."*
>
> — PROVERBS 11:13 KJV

"An unfaithful friend is like a broken foot or a broken tooth," my spiritual father said. "You can't depend on either one of them."

Sometimes, people may think that certain words won't have an impact because they were not heard. But, have you ever walked into a room and you could tell or feel someone was talking about you? Perhaps we should watch what we say when people are not around us.

Can we reap from what we speak, even when no one hears us? The Word of God states:

> *"For he that soweth to his flesh shall of the flesh reap*

corruption; but he that soweth to the Spirit
shall of the Spirit reap life everlasting."

— GALATIANS 6:8 KJV

In the same chapter, it also states:

"As we have therefore opportunity, let us do good
unto all men, especially unto them who are of
the household of faith."

— GALATIANS 6:10 KJV

What kind of words are you sowing? Are you sowing life or death with your words?

"For by thy words thou shalt be justified, and by thy
words thou shalt be condemned."

— MATTHEW 12:37 KJV

Words are powerful! Just ask the person who hears the words: "You are hired!" or "You are fired!" Words can speak truth or lies, and as a result, they can lead to lives being restored or destroyed. Words can also start a fight or even cause a war between countries.

God's words can destroy the plans of the enemy and deliver us. As we know, the Word of God is profound; as the foundation of our Christian walk, we become more and more aware of the importance of God's word in our lives. It became evident as I discovered how many other voices and words are spoken to me every day. We exist because of God's Word. The Lord commanded the world into existence by speaking. We must understand how necessary and valuable our words are.

WRITTEN WORDS

> *"A word fitly spoken is like apples of gold in pictures of silver. As an earring of gold, and an orna- ment of fine gold, so is a wise reprover upon an obedient ear. As the cold of snow in the time of harvest, so is a faithful messenger to them that send him: for he refresheth the soul of his masters."*

— PROVERBS 25:11-13 KJV

Words that are written are just as powerful as words that are spoken. For example, a doctor may write an incorrect prescrip- tion, or a person may write unkind words in a text. Both spoken and written words can positively or negatively affect a person. Therefore, we must be careful not only about what we say, but also what we write.

In our daily lives, we often see written words. A library is filled with books with written words. Tests are usually given in a written format, and instructions are written down. Schools and employment facilities have rules that are written out on documents.

During times of slavery in America, the masters didn't want those who were enslaved to learn how to read because written words would have given them access to knowledge. Written words allowed them to learn things, such as how to figure out which way to go, how to receive land, and how to read God's Word.

The written word of God is very effective. If you believe it, it will change your life. Words, whether spoken or written, have life.

> *"For verily I say unto you, Till heaven and earth*
> *pass, one jot or one tittle shall in no wise pass*
> *from the law, till all be fulfilled."*
>
> — MATTHEW 5:18 KJV

This Scripture helps us understand the impact of written words. Written words, like spoken ones, can break a person's heart or crush their spirit. Please, before you send that text, be reminded of the unintended consequences that may result.

PERSONAL REFLECTION

According to Ephesians 4:32, the Bible says we should be kind and affectionate to one another. Today, I challenge you to write a kind note to yourself or someone else the Lord places on your heart.

_____

_____

_____

_____

_____

_____

_____

_____

_____

_____

_____

_____

_____

_____

_____

_____

_____

_____

_____

_____

_____

_____

_____

NEGATIVE WORDS

The heart of the righteous studieth to answer: but
the mouth of the wicked poureth out evil things.

— PROVERBS 15:28 KJV

There are several ways that words can be used negatively to demean another person. Examples include words that are: belittling, critical, manipulative, demeaning, wicked, and hidden (or secretive).

BELITTLING WORDS

According to Lexico.com, belittling means to be "dismissive of the importance of a person or thing." The definition of dismissive means that "someone is making a person unworthy of consideration or ignoring" (Oxford Dictionary). If someone expresses themselves to another person, it is always important to take note of it like the Lord does for us. When others are talking, we need to stop and give them our undivided attention to show consideration, to acknowledge that what they're saying is important.

CRITICAL WORDS

According to Lexico.com, critical means "expressing adverse or disapproving comments or judgments." When a person is critical, they can find everything wrong and pick a person apart with words. When people are critical, they often find fault in others without first examining themselves.

> *"And why beholdest thou the mote that is in thy*
> *brother's eye, but considerest not the beam that*
> *is in thine own eye?"*
>
> — MATTHEW 7:3 KJV

MANIPULATIVE WORDS

According to Lexico.com, manipulative means "unscrupulous control of a situation or person." Some people are so clever with their words that you may begin to question yourself when they finish talking to you; this is called gaslighting. We must be aware of when this happens.

We saw how God uses words to speak the world into existence and to speak life. Now, let's examine how Satan uses manipulative words through a play on words to speak death.

> *"Now the serpent was more subtle than any beast*
> *of the field which the Lord God had made.*
> *And he said unto the woman, Yea, hath God*
> *said, Ye shall not eat of every tree of the*
> *garden?*

And the woman said unto the serpent, We may eat
of the fruit of the trees of the garden:
But of the fruit of the tree which is in the midst of
the garden, God hath said, Ye shall not eat of it,
neither shall ye touch it, lest ye die.
And the serpent said unto the woman, Ye shall not
surely die:
For God doth know that in the day ye eat thereof,
then your eyes shall be opened, and ye shall be
as gods, knowing good and evil.

— GENESIS 3:1-5 KJV

Here, we can see that Eve was reciting what God had said. She said God did not want them to eat fruit from the tree. However, Satan twisted God's words in a manipulative and cunning way. Satan said that she would not die.

Imagine having a conversation with someone, and you know what you said and your intentions. However, by the time you get through the conversation, you begin to question yourself. What you said was well-intended, but then the words were switched, giving a different meaning. Sometimes, people may twist and turn your words, which can be very cunning and destructive. To be cunning, one must be skilled and very clever, which can be very dangerous.

"Behold, I send you forth as sheep in the midst of
wolves: be ye therefore wise as serpents, and
harmless as doves."

— MATTHEW 10:16 KJV

Therefore, we must be careful with our words, especially if

we are well-spoken and knowledgeable. The Spirit of the Lord will allow you to see clearly when you're being manipulated and controlled. Looking back in the Bible to when Eve was talking to Satan, Eve was influenced by Satan's words, which changed the course of humanity.

PUT-DOWNS

According to Lexico.com, put-downs are "a remark intended to humiliate or criticize someone." They're acts or expressions that show scorn and are usually intended to hurt another person's feelings. Put-downs are little jabs with words.

There is a difference between a joke and disrespect disguised as a joke. For example, someone may see a person and make a lighthearted joke about their appearance. Both individuals may find it to be funny and laugh. Laughter is good and can be healthy. Nevertheless, a joke can go too far if an individual insults or disrespects somebody that another individual cares about. This can cause an adverse reaction. Putting people down in front of others, insulting them, and picking on them is embarrassing to the person being talked about.

In actuality, people who do this bring attention to themselves. While putting someone else down, they attract attention because their actions are so cruel. It allows others to see who that person is on the inside. Put-downs may be spoken by close friends and family members. However, focus on the good instead of finding faults or putting others down. In the event that corrections are needed, this should always be done in private.

Words are very powerful and can even cause rejection. In the book, "Keys to Healing Rejection," the author Marilyn Hickey asserts, "rejection comes from words." When somebody speaks negatively to you, it wounds your personality and spirit, making you feel rejected. Fundamentally, rejection stems from hurtful words. Have you ever had someone come up to you and ask, "Do you know what I have heard about you?" Negative words hurt deeply.

Rejection also manifests in behavior; it's how a person acts toward another person. An anonymous writer once wrote: "Train your mind to hear what God whispers and not what the enemy shouts!" Don't allow other negative opinions to consume your soul.

Rejection and the silent treatment are forms of emotional abuse. Not talking to someone for days is a method to train or punish someone. It is controlling and manipulative. It uses psychology by making people look at themselves inwardly and question if it's their fault. The silent treatment is worse than someone calling you a name because it's a mental attack.

> *"Keep thy heart with all diligence; for out of it are the issues of life."*
>
> — PROVERBS 4:23 KJV

Words are first developed as thoughts, and we must train our minds to think the way Christ thinks, based on the Word of God. Your mind should be the same as that of Jesus Christ. Therefore, we should strive daily to ensure that our mind is the same as the mind of Christ.

> *"Let this mind be in you, which was also in Christ Jesus."*
>
> — PHILIPPIANS 2:5 KJV

WICKED WORDS

According to the dictionary, wicked means "intended to or capable of harming someone or something." Other words (synonyms) that mean the same are: evil, sinful, immoral, wrong, wrongful, and bad. Wicked words are the opposite of what God desires. God desires our words and thoughts to be pure, kind, and sweet.

> *"How sweet are thy words unto my taste! Yea,*
> *sweeter than honey to my mouth!"*
>
> — PSALM 119:103 KJV

The enemy desires to use words to be wicked and evil. Often, wicked words are inspired by demonic spirits to hurt and harm others.

> *"Speak not evil one of another, brethren. He that*
> *speaketh evil of his brother, and judgeth his*
> *brother, speaketh evil of the law, and judgeth*
> *the law: but if thou judge the law, thou art not a*
> *doer of the law, but a judge."*
>
> — JAMES 4:11 KJV

Our words can either heal or harm people. Every day we can choose to bring healing to someone with a kind word. Because words contain power, they should be used to bring life. This is true because God spoke the first words of creation.

> *"For the word of God is quick, and powerful, and*
> *sharper than any two-edged sword, piercing*

38

even to the dividing asunder of soul and spirit,
and of the joints and marrow, and is a discerner
of the thoughts and intents of the heart."

— HEBREWS 4:12 KJV

Once a word (good or bad) is said, it can sometimes linger for days and even years. This validates just how powerful words are. Do you realize know how powerful our prayers are? Our prayers are composed of words; our prayers are eternal. Our prayers can manifest years later. Now that's powerful! God can use our words (prayers) to answer prayers.

The Word of God is quick, powerful, and sharp. Imagine how our words can be similar to others, at times. Have you ever heard an adult talk about what their parents said to them when they were a child? A man or woman can remember what their sweetheart said years ago. The list of examples is long. Therefore, it is essential to note that these examples illustrate how words can have a long-lasting effect. It ultimately takes the power of God to repair brokenness from words. The Lord knew we would need His Word and the Holy Spirit to receive healing from the brokenness of the world we live in.

"To speak evil of no man, to be no brawlers, but
gentle, shewing all meekness unto all men. For
we ourselves also were sometimes foolish,
disobedient, deceived, serving divers lusts and
pleasures, living in malice and envy, hateful,
and hating one another."

— TITUS 3:2-3 KJV

God is love and His Word is altogether lovely. When God

39

entrusts us with others who are broken, we are to value and guard them. That's why Jesus Christ is the most trustworthy friend. We've heard a popular saying in the Body of Christ: "Tell God your sorrows and people your joy, but in our human faults, we find our self-confidence in people in flesh."

> *"Thus saith the Lord; Cursed be the man that trusteth in man, and maketh flesh his arm, and whose heart departeth from the Lord."*
>
> — JEREMIAH 17:5 KJV

This is serious to God. We must put our trust in God over man. The Lord never intended for us to put our complete trust in anyone but Him, as we are all flawed and imperfect. The Holy Scriptures reveal that we all have sinned and fallen short of God's glory.

> *"For all have sinned, and come short of the glory of God."*
>
> — ROMANS 3:23 KJV

We must be careful not to break others with our words when we are broken. We must trust the Lord to heal our brokenness with His words.

Steve Harvey, a famous comedian, reflected on a time when he was in school. When his teacher told everyone to write down what they wanted to be as a grown-up, Mr. Harvey said, "I want to be on television." So, the teacher asked him, "Why would you put that down?" The teacher asked this because Mr. Harvey had a stuttering condition at that time. As we know, Mr. Harvey went on to be very successful as a comedian and in other roles on television. Yes, he was able to overcome an obstacle. But the point is that he never forgot his teacher's words, as he could still recount that moment. Mr. Harvey even sent his teacher a television to show how the Lord had blessed his life. Mr. Harvey's teacher's words were so powerful that I believe they contributed to his perseverance.

Steve Harvey's story could have been different. The teacher's words could have discouraged him from never moving forward or giving up. Therefore, it's important to understand that teachers, pastors, parents, companions, friends, and anyone you value can play a major part in your life through their words. Words from people in authority are especially powerful; they have the ability to transform or destroy someone's life if the person values their words. Thanks be unto God our heavenly Father, for He is the ultimate authority, and has the final say!

PERSONAL REFLECTION

According to Ephesians 4:29, the Bible says, "Let no corrupt communication proceed out of your mouth, but that which is good to the use of edifying, that it may minister grace unto the hearers." Today, I challenge you to identify every negative word used against you, cancel it out, and replace it with the Word of God.

_____

_____

_____

_____

_____

_____

_____

_____

_____

_____

_____

_____

_____

_____

_____

_____

_____

_____

_____

_____

_____

_____

_____

_____

SHERITA C. WHITE

VERBALLY ABUSIVE WORDS

Verbal abuse is underestimated and can create an unhealthy environment. It can also be very deceptive. It always starts out as quite the opposite. In the beginning, the words are usually smooth and sweet, so you won't recognize them until you become deeply involved.

> *"The words of his mouth were smoother than butter, but war was in his heart: his words were softer than oil, yet were they drawn swords."*
>
> — PSALM 55:21 KJV

Verbally abusive words can drain the life out of a person. Verbal abuse is real; it is exhausting and draining. People calling you names such as: crazy, stupid, schizophrenic, bipolar, and other derogatory names are very dangerous and unhealthy. This kind of environment is challenging and nearly impossible to thrive in. Verbally abusive words can hurt more than a fist. A person can heal externally faster than internally from these types of words being spoken over them for years.

I once heard a man of God teach that verbal abuse is a precursor to physical abuse. This means that if a person has a problem speaking to others in a demeaning way, it could easily lead to physical aggression. Verbal abusers can drain your emotions and be considered narcissistic because they attack every part of a person and cause the person being abused to overthink and believe that it's always their fault. Just know this: it is not your fault! The abuser will also say such things as: "It's your imagination," "You're being too sensitive," "You have issues," "You need help," "You just keep it going," and "Here we go again," to make you feel like you're making things up. Take courage. We are overcomers.

> *"I can do all things through Christ which strengtheneth me."*
>
> — PHILIPPIANS 4:13 KJV

How is it possible that the same mouth that blessed you cursed you (James 3:10)? Well, one thing is that we are human. Second, Bishop Daniel M. Jordan always says, "We have to die some more!" In other words, we have to ask the Holy Spirit to let us operate in the gifts of the Spirit, and one of the gifts is self-control.

> *"But the fruit of the Spirit is love, joy, peace, longsuffering, gentleness, goodness, faith..."*
>
> — GALATIANS 5:22 KJV

I know, sometimes we just want to say, "But the Holy Spirit

can help us not to say it." The hardest thing to do is not say anything. We tear each other down because we want to defend ourselves. We don't want to allow someone to speak negatively about us.

Now, there comes a time when we must speak up. The Bible says there is a time for everything; there's "a time to keep silence, and a time to speak" (Ecclesiastes 3:7 KJV). It goes back again to the heart. Only the Lord can see our hearts and reveal a person's heart. It is easy to be deceived by kind and sweet words, but what someone says is the true essence of a person.

> *"O generation of vipers, how can ye, being evil,*
> *speak good things? for out of the abundance of*
> *the heart the mouth speaketh."*
>
> — MATTHEW 12:34 KJV

Lexico.com defines evil as "profound immorality and wickedness, especially when regarded as a supernatural force." Verbally abusive words are evil pronouncements that curse and change someone's life. Verbal attacks are often demonic, especially when substance abuse is involved. With substance abuse, the person can allow the enemy to take over them. The enemy will make a person use their words to hurt, destroy, and kill others.

> *"The thief cometh not, but for to steal, and to kill,*
> *and to destroy: I am come that they might have*
> *life, and that they might have it more*
> *abundantly."*
>
> — JOHN 10:10 KJV

No matter the nature of the verbal attack, abuse is not okay. It's essential to understand and protect your worth. We must cancel out every word against us, such as name-calling and subtle unkind statements. Begin to plead the Blood of Jesus over you and speak the Word. Ask the Lord for strength to remove yourself from toxic environments. When a person speaks evil, we must denounce it because it's wicked.

> *"And the tongue is a fire, a world of iniquity: so is the tongue among our members, that it defileth the whole body, and setteth on fire the course of nature; and it is set on fire of hell. For every kind of beasts, and of birds, and of serpents, and of things in the sea, is tamed, and hath been tamed of mankind: But the tongue can no man tame; it is an unruly evil, full of deadly poison."*
>
> — JAMES 3:6-8 KJV

Medically, a poison is a substance capable of causing an illness or death when introduced to a living organism. Evil, demonic words have the potential to cause sickness, just like poison. All types of ailments begin to appear, such as headaches and anxiety, due to an unhealthy environment. At times, it can be difficult to control our tongue, but we know the effects that our tongue can cause. Therefore, we should be careful about what we speak, especially to those we are in fellowship with.

> *"For it was not an enemy that reproached me; then I could have borne it: neither was it he that hated me that did magnify himself against me;*

then I would have hid myself from him: But it
was thou, a man mine equal, my guide, and
mine acquaintance. We took sweet counsel
together, and walked unto the house of God in
company."

— PSALM 55:12-14 KJV

There must be both a natural and spiritual response to verbal abuse, otherwise, the verbal abuser will become comfortable with saying anything to you and all respect will be lost.

"If any man among you seem to be religious, and
bridleth not his tongue, but deceiveth his own
heart, this man's religion is vain."

— JAMES 1:26 KJV

It's not a good idea to say whatever we want, especially when angry. The Word of God can heal, deliver, and set us free from all curses and verbal abuse. God's Word can do it! Evil words are deadly. They can damage marriages and separate friendships. The Lord created us by speaking life into us. So, we are meant to receive words that build us up, not tear us down.

When spoken, evil words will cause serious contention in any relationship. Therefore, sometimes it's better not to say anything at all. However, kind words can build and heal a broken relationship. We were not designed to experience verbal abuse, or any abuse for that matter.

We can often overlook and downplay verbal abuse because it's not seen with the visible eye, like hitting. Verbal abuse can be just as destructive as physical abuse, and many times, it can linger longer than physical abuse.

Verbal abuse can be given and received by men, women, and even children. Unfortunately, our children say all kinds of mean things to each other, and sometimes even to adults. Verbal attacks are meant to attack your mental state of mind and self-esteem.

Words can make someone feel a certain way and have a certain effect. For instance, you may have initially been happy until someone said something. After hearing what they said, it may have caused you to feel sad. That's how words change someone's feelings and mood, if allowed.

Verbal abuse can be used as a way to control a person, causing a person to do whatever possible to avoid the possibility of a confrontation. Verbal abuse can cause fear and paralyze the person being victimized.

Consider the following prayer from the *Red Prayer Book*:

> I ask You, Lord, to destroy all demonic spirits that have been sent forth from those words and/or prayers and cast them into the abyss, along with those words, the power of those words and/or prayers, pain, darkness, darts, arrows, stings, claws, spears, lies, evil imprints, impressions, false memories, and wrong mindsets, throughout the rest of this day into tomorrow afternoon. Amen.
>
> — CHRISTIAN WORD MINISTRIES

Verbally abusive words can be a silent killer. They can kill you from the inside out. You may ask: "Why would you call it a silent killer?" It's because you can surround yourself with others, and no one can see the scars on the inside of you that's screaming for help. Physical scars can heal, but verbal scars can take years to heal. People can move on in life after physically removing themselves from a verbally abusive situation. However, even a small word can still trigger them. That's how strong words are. But the Word of God is stronger!

The funny thing about verbal abuse is that the person verbally abusing another may not think it's a big deal. Maybe, they may even feel like the person deserved it. However, you can almost forget who you are if you hear belittling words, judgmental, and critical words. It may begin to weigh on you, emotionally.

One of my sisters in Christ told me a story about a man. One day, the man's mother told him he was a mistake, and the grown man broke down and cried like a baby. That's why the Lord shows us how powerful words are. We must pray before we say things; pray before you say!

Let's look at how Solomon spoke kindly. The book of Song of Solomon contains the most beautiful words. No wonder Solomon had so many wives in his time; he had about 700 wives and 300 concubines. The one thing we know about Solomon is that he knew how to speak sweet, kind words.

> *"Tell me, O thou whom my soul loveth... O thou fairest among women... O my love... Thy cheeks are comely with rows of jewels, thy neck with chains of gold... Behold, thou art fair, my love; behold, thou art fair; thou hast doves' eyes."*
>
> — SONG OF SOLOMON 1:7-15 KJV

Verbal abuse can come from different sources. We hear it all the time on television, through social media platforms, and even in our homes. According to the online medical website, WebMD, verbal abuse (also known as emotional abuse) is "a range of words or behaviors used to manipulate, intimidate, and maintain power and control over someone." WebMD also includes examples such as, "insults, humiliation and ridicule, the silent treatment, and attempts to scare, isolate, and control."

If a person can't control another person, the best way to attack them is to degrade them with name-calling, put-downs, and insults; sometimes, it could be in a cute, condescending way. For example, someone might downplay another person's accomplishments by saying, "Aren't you the one with the college education?" It can be a very small thing you want to share, and a person might say, "Oh, I know someone else who can do that, and it didn't take them that long." They may say that because they do not value you or your accomplishments. Verbal abuse can come in various forms. However, one thing is for sure; it will always come through words. Verbal abuse can also cause fear when you don't know what will set the verbal abuser off.

When verbal attacks come, we can live by them, refuse them, replace them, or accept them. One tool to defend yourself against verbal attacks is positive affirmations. You can use your journal to write down everything the Lord says you are!

Verbal attacks can start with arguments over the most minor things. Here's a little humor for my sisters in Christ. Let's look at the Book of Proverbs, which talks about a quarrelsome wife. I asked the Lord why He did not mention quarrelsome men because some men are cankerous and even more argumentative than women. Scripture states, "It is better to dwell in the wilderness, than with a contentious and an angry woman" (Proverbs 21:19 KJV). It's not fun to be around a person who is constantly nagging. That speaks volumes if you have peace when that person is not around. Peace is truly a blessing. The Lord wants us to have peace in our homes, minds, and heart. Our prayer is for the Lord to give us peace.

> *"Peace I leave with you, my peace I give unto you: not as the world giveth, give I unto you. Let not your heart be troubled, neither let it be afraid."*
>
> — JOHN 14:27 KJV

One important thing to note is that we can't fight the tongue on our own without the help of the Holy Spirit, because the tongue can get out of control. Once you override the Holy Spirit and go ahead and say something, conviction comes. As Believers, we are supposed to have self-control with the help of the Lord. What you say can reveal your true identity. As I am writing, I am asking the Holy Spirit to help because some people are sent by the enemy to use words that disturb our peace.

The Lord can and will deliver us from every situation if you ask Him. The Holy Spirit will guide us through life because He is a precious gift to the Body of Christ.

> *"What shall we then say to these things? If God be for us, who can be against us?" "I cried unto God with my voice, even unto God with my voice; and he gave ear unto me."*
>
> — ROMANS 8:31 KJV

Cry out for help from verbal abuse and ask God to be healed of any emotional trauma. It's a process, but it can be done with His help!

> *"I cried unto God with my voice, even unto God with my voice; and he gave ear unto me."*
>
> — PSALM 77:1 KJV

If you bring all of your concerns to the Holy Spirit, He will fight for and help you. Jesus is our answer to every situation we face.

> *"God is our refuge and strength, a very present help in trouble."*
>
> — PSALM 46:1 KJV

God's Word can heal us. Nothing can stand a chance against our Almighty God.

> *"What shall we then say to these things? If God be for us, who can be against us?"*
>
> — ROMANS 8:31 KJV

HIDDEN WORDS

The home is where we are most comfortable and relaxed. However, we must be careful because the Lord sees and hears all things that go on, even behind closed doors. We behave unseemly when we begin to hide things in our homes. None of us are perfect. When we hide something, this is how the enemy comes in and creates confusion and chaos, eventually breaking down the family.

Privacy is absolutely necessary for our lives and families. However, we should address and deal with issues. Family meetings and prayer can be effective strategies to use. Our homes should be a place of peace, not a war zone! Hidden things lead to secrets. When we reveal it to God, He can begin to work.

> *"For nothing is hidden that will not be made manifest, nor is anything secret that will not be known and come to light."*
>
> — LUKE 8:17 KJV

SECRETS IN THE HOUSE

According to Oxford Language, a secret is something that is kept or meant to be kept unknown to others. Things are happening within our homes that should not be happening.

Within Christian homes, there should be love and peace. However, the enemy tries to kill and destroy the family because he knows that if the family can unite, they can be victorious and help others come to the Lord. So, that's why we see families struggling with divorce, alcohol, profanity, adultery, fornication, and other unhealthy behaviors.

The enemy uses secrets to bring shame, which fosters feelings of condemnation. The well-known pastor, Bishop TD Jakes, produced a movie entitled "Woman Thou Art Loosed." The film depicted a young girl who was sexually assaulted; when the girl told her mother, the mother accused the girl of being provocative, but that wasn't the case. The daughter was telling the truth.

In many of our homes, there are secrets. We must bring things to the Lord so our families can be delivered. We shouldn't hide our family pain. We need to surrender it to God so He can deliver the family. Many times, physical, verbal, and sexual abuse starts in the home. The enemy tells us to keep it a secret.

Sometimes, people continue to stay in toxic homes for various reasons. It may be due to financial reasons, appearance, or guilt. Also, it could be that the individual is struggling with loneliness, desperation, or fear of the unknown; they may not be able to take care of themselves and their children.

Many families are destroyed because of secrets, shame, lies, and cover-ups. The Lord loves healthy and whole families. He never intended for families to be dysfunctional or torn apart. Families must fight to be made whole from discord and strife in the home because the enemy has another plan contrary to God's. (John 10:10). The enemy fights families because healthy families make healthy churches; where there is unity, there is strength (Deuteronomy 32:30).

Once we take it to the Lord, He will allow other resources, such as therapy and our trusted church leaders, to guide us and pray for our families. However, the whole family unit has to be willing to put the work in to be successful. Rest assured, Jesus is a trusted friend. He is the best secret keeper there is! He won't tell anyone. The best part is that He will deliver and set us free.

> *"If the Son therefore shall make you free, ye shall be free indeed."*
>
> — JOHN 8:36 KJV

Only Jesus can do that!

YELLING

The reality is we all may have yelled or been yelled at. Let's examine its effects.

Yelling is a behavior that often surfaces when a person is angry. An angry person tends to yell because it's a natural response. Yelling and anger go hand-in-hand because both command attention.

In most situations, yelling is negative unless you're cheering for your team or someone at a sporting event. In other situations, yelling and shouting can be necessary to get someone's attention. Nonetheless, yelling can be damaging in any relationship. Yelling sometimes involves hurtful, destructive words, as it generally comes from a place of being angry and frustrated. As a result, yelling can cause a person to want to remove themselves from another person's presence to avoid strife and contention.

Anger is a dangerous emotion. If a person's anger is left unchecked, it can damage all those around them emotionally and physically. Let's look at one of the Lord's servants. Saved people have issues, too. Honestly, the best Christians to be around are genuine ones that know that if it had not been for the Lord, they would have been a mess. We are all a work in progress!

Let's look at Moses and how he demonstrated his anger.

> *"And it came to pass, as soon as he came nigh unto the camp, that he saw the calf, and the dancing: and Moses' anger waxed hot, and he cast the tables out of his hands, and brake them beneath the mount."*

Although Moses was humble, he still dealt with anger. Instead of delivering God's Word, he threw the tablets out of frustration. This is how anger can keep you from receiving God's purpose and plan.

When we are angry, it's tough to be quiet, so we usually vent our anger. Anger can make a person foolish and lose the ability to reason.

Did you know that the Lord gets angry?

> *"And the anger of the Lord was kindled against*
> *Moses, and he said, Is not Aaron the Levite thy*
> *brother? I know that he can speak well. And*
> *also, behold, he cometh forth to meet thee: and*
> *when he seeth thee, he will be glad in his heart."*

— EXODUS 4:14 KJV

I don't know about you, but I would rather the Lord be angry with me than have other people angry with me. Why? The Lord has more grace and mercy than some people, even when He's angry.

One way to diffuse our anger is to confess it to the Lord; He will remove it because Jesus is the answer to our bitterness.

> *"Follow peace with all men, and holiness, without*
> *which no man shall see the Lord: Looking dili-*
> *gently lest any man fail of the grace of God; lest*

any root of bitterness springing up trouble you,
and thereby many be defiled."

— HEBREWS 12:14-15

Sometimes, we become angry with the Lord because of things that occurred in our lives, but the Lord is still faithful and knows what's best for us. We should still love Him, even when we don't get our way. We will understand it better by and by. We may throw our fits and temper tantrums like children, but He still loves us. We serve such a loving and forgiving God. If we want to be free from anger, we need the Holy Spirit to help us. He can handle the most minor issues, even ones you think are insignificant. He can surely help with significant issues like anger.

"Be not hasty in thy spirit to be angry: for anger
resteth in the bosom of fools."

— ECCLESIASTES 7:9 KJV

The root cause of anger includes fear, pain, frustration, irritation, abuse, and unfairness. Anger is a stronghold to keep a person from forgiving. Anger is not a sin; we naturally become angry when treated unfairly or unjustly. However, when anger turns into aggression, this can lead a person to sin. If anger is held onto, it can cause a person to act foolish.

"Be ye angry, and sin not: let not the sun go down
upon your wrath."

— EPHESIANS 4:26 KJV

What is the difference between anger and wrath? In brief, anger is a strong feeling of annoyance, displeasure, or hostility, while wrath is an extreme form of anger. Anger is a natural emotion that always involves violence, vengeance, and destruction. People are very dangerous when they seek to kill and destroy anything and anyone in their path out of revenge and resentment.

> *"Dearly beloved, avenge not yourselves, but rather give place unto wrath: for it is written, Vengeance is mine; I will repay, saith the Lord. Therefore, if thine enemy hunger, feed him; if he thirst, give him drink: for in so doing thou shalt heap coals of fire on his head. Be not overcome of evil, but overcome evil with good."*
>
> — ROMANS 12:19-21 KJV

So, yes, yelling out of anger can lead to evil and harm. It consists of not only the sound of being loud, but also the choice of words. It can even be associated with fear. According to Merriam-Webster, yelling means "to give a loud, sharp cry; to cry out; to call out; to scream; or to shout." Similar to yelling is shouting. According to the Oxford Language, shouting means to "utter a loud call or cry, typically as an expression of strong emotions."

Yelling can affect everyone. Examples include: customers yelling, a parent yelling at a child, or a couple yelling in front of a child. Yelling also can make one feel unsafe and uncomfortable. For instance, when parents yell at children, one may view it as abuse.

Is yelling the best way to express yourself? Absolutely not! Actually, yelling does the opposite and does not restore. It causes a person to withdraw and dismiss themselves from the situation. Yelling is loud and produces words that evoke various emotions.

A 2014 research study in the "Journal of Child Development" shows that yelling produces results similar to physical punishment in children. Results from this experiment showed that children who were yelled at had increased levels of anxiety, stress, depression, and an increase in behavioral problems. Another study showed that if one is yelled at enough, it changes their mind, brain, and body. Yelling can be used as a weapon and is a form of verbal abuse. Yelling can even lead to stress and emotional disorders. Those children can grow up becoming depressed and emotionally stressed adults.

If a person yells at you, it may bring about fear and anxiety. Yelling is dangerous; it is a form of mental and physiological abuse. It can cause depression, low self-esteem, and suicidal thoughts. Yelling can even cause a person to question what they did wrong, which is another form of control. Yelling can also break someone's spirit. You may have heard the saying: "It's not what you say, but how you say it." Actually, it is precisely what you say and how loud you say it. All that mattered was that it had a profound effect on a person.

Yelling can take the form of a loud voice that negatively impacts the atmosphere. A person's voice can express a certain tone, whether it be one of concern, disgust, sarcasm, or excitement. One's tone of voice can manifest a change in the environment. As hard as it may seem, the only thing that can shut down yelling is the opposite, talking in a calm voice. However, when a person continues to yell, it causes others to yell in response.

When someone says something to you in a soft tone, it is easier to receive that rather than someone yelling and screaming. It can be hard to process what a person is saying when they're yelling, and the only person that may hear you is you. Even if the person is right in what they're saying, it stirs up anger and can become grievous.

> *"A soft answer turneth away wrath: but grievous words stir up anger."*
>
> — PROVERBS 15:1 KJV

Therefore, we must be careful not to yell and watch the tone of how we address people in anger.

Both yelling and the tone of a person's voice carry a spirit and a sound. According to the Oxford Language, a sound is the "vibration that travels through the air or another medium and can be heard when they reach a person's or animal's ear."

Tones can be demonstrated through music and even through writing. Storytelling can set the tone of a story, and a person can set the tone of how they speak at events. For example, at a church service, people can become excited by the tone of the pastor's voice. A person doesn't have to yell, but the way or manner in which they speak can be perceived through a tone. You can tell by someone's tone if they are happy or displeased. It's a sound!

For instance, when you're calling a company concerning business, you can tell how the conversation will go just by the sound and tone of the person's voice. In customer service, you can almost immediately tell by a person's tone how they are feeling. You can tell they are angry or upset if they shout and curse. If their voice sounds soft and pleasant, they may be laid back.

*"Set a watch, O Lord, before my mouth; keep the
door of my lips."*

— PSALM 141:3 KJV

*Lord, help us to refrain from yelling and help us to watch our tones
when speaking to others. Deliver us from anger and bitterness.*

PERSONAL REFLECTION

The Bible says, "Let no corrupt communication proceed out of your mouth, but that which is good to the use of edifying, that it may minister grace unto the hearers." (Ephesians 4:29 KJV). Today, I challenge you to look at ways you can stop yourself from yelling. Ask yourself these questions: "How will I react to this situation?" or "What issues will arise if I raise my voice?" Praying and keeping a journal are some alternatives to prevent yelling.

_____

_____

_____

_____

_____

_____

_____

_____

_____

_____

_____

_____

_____

_____

_____

_____

_____

_____

_____

_____

POSITIVE WORDS

CONSTRUCTIVE CRITICISM

According to the Oxford Dictionary, constructive means "serving a useful purpose" and "tending to build-up." As defined on Element Three's website, constructive criticism is "the process of offering valid and well-reasoned opinions about the work of others, usually involving both positive and negative comments, in a friendly manner rather than an oppositional one."

Collaboration often involves constructive criticism as a means of raising performance standards and maintaining them. However, when receiving constructive criticism, some people become defensive, because it may either be overused or sound negative.

A study was conducted by researchers on two animals to test the impact of words. Every day, they spoke kindly to one animal, and as a result, that animal flourished and was happy. On the other hand, they yelled and screamed at another animal; consequently, that animal ran, hid, and later became ill. Considering that animals can be influenced by words and tones, imagine what people might experience. I pray that the Lord helps us to remember how powerful words are before we speak.

PROPHETIC WORDS

Throughout my Christian walk, I have received prophetic words concerning my life from individuals personally and from preachers over the pulpit. Prophetic words are very powerful and should never be taken lightly. It's a precious gift through the Holy Spirit.

Over the years, I've always wondered about some of the words I received. Some words have been a blessing to me, and I've written them down to see if they would come to pass. Other words spoken have caused me to go away feeling worse than when I came to the service.

A prophetic Word is not something to be taken lightly, and must be used with care and caution.

> *"For the time will come when they will not endure sound doctrine; but after their own lusts shall they heap to themselves teachers, having itching ears."*
>
> — 2 TIMOTHY 4:3

Many years ago, a woman of God prophesied over me. When I left that service, I was crying and scared at the same time, as this was my introduction to the prophetic ministry. I did not fully understand what was happening at the time. I took everything to heart, but a seasoned man of God told me that I needed to discern the words that I was given.

To determine if prophetic words are from the Lord, we can take them to Him. If it's a Word from God, it will fall in line with what He has already been dealing with you privately about. Then, you will see how everything comes to pass later. Furthermore, it is possible for us to miss it and speak from the flesh. There are two things I have learned in my Christian experience; the first is that not everyone should pray over you or prophesy to you. The second thing is that discernment is very important.

"And the king of Israel said unto Jehoshaphat,
'There is yet one man, by whom we may
enquire of the Lord: but I hate him; for he never
prophesied good unto me, but always evil.'"

— 2 CHRONICLES 18:7A KJV

The Lord wants us to try to spirit by the spirit, which means we must cross-check or carefully examine prophetic words. Even prophetic words should be gauged by the Word of God. Just like we cannot receive every word in the natural realm, we must discern the prophetic by the Word of God.

It's also important to remember that God may not show everything to the person who is prophesying. I had a personal experience where I struggled to make a life-changing decision. So, I asked the individual to agree with me in prayer regarding the situation. As they were praying, a Word came from the Lord, giving me divine instruction. I knew this person had heard from God, but I still struggled with the decision. So, I went to the Lord and said, "God I know this person hears from you, but I want you to tell me what to do."

"For we know in part, and we prophesy in part. But

> *when that which is perfect is come, then that*
> *which is in part shall be done away."*

> — 1 CORINTHIANS 13:9-10 KJV

In the situation I faced, my personal decision was based on the guidance and direction of the Holy Spirit, using God's Word as a guidepost. This is why God's Word is so important; it will guide you. The Lord admonishes us,"

> *"Then the Lord said unto me, The prophets*
> *prophesy lies in my name: I sent them not,*
> *neither have I commanded them, neither spake*
> *unto them: they prophesy unto you a false*
> *vision and divination, and a thing of nought,*
> *and the deceit of their heart."*

> — JEREMIAH 4:14 KJV

All prophetic words are not from the Lord.

SENSITIVE WORDS

All my life, I have been told by others that I am sensitive. I understand it can be hard to reveal some of our flaws because they can be used against us. However, it can also be liberating because the Lord can heal you when you confess your issues.

> *"If we confess our sins, he is faithful and just to*
> *forgive us our sins, and to cleanse us from all*
> *unrighteousness."*

> — 1 JOHN 1:9 KJV

Is sensitivity a sin? No, I don't believe so. In my opinion, people are not always sensitive. Sometimes people are just harsh, lacking gentleness and compassion. They may deny this and try to label you as having the problem.

Whenever we are in the presence of the Lord, we leave feeling better than when we entered; His presence brings joy and peace.

> *"Thou wilt shew me the path of life: in thy presence is fulness of joy; at thy right hand there are pleasures for evermore."*
>
> — PSALM 16:11 KJV

Although He corrects us, He does it in a tender, loving way. One way to check if you're being too sensitive is to pay attention to how a conversation makes you feel. I know we must be careful with feelings, but pay attention to the point at which you feel hurt and defensive in a conversation. When someone truly tries to speak to you from a loving place, they will approach you with care because love covers. Sometimes, though, when a person has deep wounds, they may hear things differently than what was intended. Bishop Daniel M. Jordan, my spiritual father in Gospel, always taught me to build people up before correcting them. It's good to tell them what they did right before telling them what they did wrong. By showing them love first, they are better able to receive your correction.

Sensitivity is not necessarily a bad thing. Having sensitivity means being attentive to other people's feelings or being thoughtful, no matter the situation. In our dealings with others and with the Lord, we should be sensitive and thought-ful. Being sensitive to the Holy Spirit is a good thing. For example, this can happen when the Lord corrects us. God knows our personalities. He speaks to us in a way that we can understand. Perhaps you can recall a time when another person could have said what they said to you at a different time or in a different way. We shouldn't always speak our minds whenever we feel like it. We are all imperfect. But we should try to be considerate of others and their feelings. It is a common misconception that a person is sensitive when in fact the other individual is being unkind with their words. The reality is that they may have addressed you in a rude or mean way. The Holy Spirit is sensitive. Therefore, we should all be sensitive and kind to others.

"And grieve not the Holy Spirit of God."

— EPHESIANS 4:30 KJV

This Scripture is so powerful because it proves that the Holy Spirit is a person and we can grieve Him with our words, thoughts, and actions. The Holy Spirit is a person; therefore, He can experience grief and sorrow. Therefore, we must always be careful with what we say.

"Pleasant words are as an honeycomb, sweet to the soul, and health to the bones."

— PROVERBS 16:24 KJV

Therefore, we should never cause another person to feel afraid or defensive; we should use kind words. Kind words are like honey; honey is sweet. In nature, honey has a wide range of natural benefits, from heart health to wound healing. Likewise, kind words are healthy for the body; evil words are unhealthy for the body and the mind.

THE PREACHED WORD OF GOD

The preached Word is simply amazing! A powerful message over the pulpit can change a sinner or a Believer's life.

> *"For after that in the wisdom of God the world by wisdom knew not God, it pleased God by the foolishness of preaching to save them that believe."*

> — 1 CORINTHIANS 1:21 KJV

What's so amazing about the Word of God is that when it's preached under the anointing, a sinner can feel the power of God through the preacher's words.

> *"Preach the word; be instant in season, out of season; reprove, rebuke, exhort with all longsuffering and doctrine."*

> — 2 TIMOTHY 4:2 KJV

The Word of God changes your mind and attitude while hearing the preached Word. The preached Word can give you hope and transform your life. The preached Word is very powerful; it can and will deliver you.

If a person is called to the ministry to minister the Word, it is always good to seek a Word from the Lord for the people. This is very important because the preached Word of God can save a life and encourage someone to hold on. In the words of my Spiritual Father Bishop Daniel M. Jordan, "always be led by the Holy Spirit."

TRUSTING WORDS

We build trust with our words and actions. Trust starts with our words. For example, if you tell someone that you will meet them at the library at 5:00 pm and then show up, that person will see you as someone who keeps their word. However, if something comes up and you can no longer make it on time, you can tell the person that you may be running 15 minutes behind. As a result of doing that, you can build trust because you communicated to let that person know. This pattern of behavior should even extend to children. When we tell them that we will do something, we should do everything in our power to follow through with it because it's all about building trust. Parents can hurt their children by not keeping their word.

> *"He swears to his own hurt and does not change."*
>
> — PSALM 15:4B NASB

Sometimes, we may accidentally breach our trust with the same people who placed their trust in us, instead of restoring them. This is how the words "brokenness" and "broken" are brought about.

According to the Oxford Dictionary, broken means "having been fractured or damaged and no longer in one piece." When people feel broken by negative words, they feel an emotional pain that stops them from living a normal healthy life. Being broken by words is two-folded. It is not only the person hearing the negative words who may be broken, but also the one speaking them. This is why we must put our total trust in the Lord.

*"Trust in the Lord with all thine heart; and lean not
unto thine own understanding. In all thy ways
acknowledge him, and he shall direct thy
paths."*

— PROVERBS 3:5-6 KJV

PERSONAL REFLECTION

It's important to speak life about ourselves and our situations. We must not confess the negative thoughts that may be in our mind. Rather, we must speak life by faith. So, today, I want to challenge you to write down some positive things about yourself and others that will bring life.

_____

_____

_____

_____

_____

_____

_____

_____

_____

_____

_____

_____

_____

_____

_____

_____

_____

_____

_____

_____

_____

_____

_____

SHERITA C. WHITE

WORDS OF FORGIVENESS

"And I heard a loud voice saying in heaven, Now is come salvation, and strength, and the kingdom of our God, and the power of his Christ: for the accuser of our brethren is cast down, which accused them before our God day and night."

— REVELATION 12:10 KJV

In the words of my spiritual father in the Gospel, Bishop Daniel M. Jordan, "People see you fall, but they never see you get up!" That's how the enemy comes to accuse us— through the things we have and have not done. Whatever the accusation is, God knows that the enemy would come to accuse God's children. Jesus became an advocate for his children and is a forgiver of sins.

*"If we confess our sins, he is faithful and just to
forgive us our sins, and to cleanse us from all
unrighteousness."*

— 1 JOHN 1:9 KJV

*"And he is the propitiation for our sins: and not for
ours only, but also for the sins of the whole
world."*

— 1 JOHN 2:2 KJV

Accusation and forgiveness coincide together. These two words coexist because when people accuse, they are proving you're wrong. Once that happens, you have to forgive the person for the accusation, right or wrong. Forgiveness is a part of life that's unavoidable, even if we want to avoid it. It is a requirement from the Lord, and it's mentioned in God's Word many times. You may think to yourself: "If I forgive them, there is a possibility that they will hurt me again." But you have to trust the Lord to help you and ask Him to show you that you can trust that person. Some people really do change and mean well, and the Lord knows the hearts of each individual. There are people who never apologize or are never given the opportunity to apologize. It is a blessing if God gives you this chance.

People have served time in prison because of accusations, whether they are guilty or not. The enemy tries to put you in a prison of guilt, regrets, and shame. Accusing someone is like imprisoning someone. An accusation is binding and is a way to keep a person held hostage to whatever sin they may or may not have committed. Satan is the accuser of the brethren. If we accuse others, we take on the characteristics of Satan; but God did not come to condemn us. Instead, He came to save us. When we forgive, we take on the characteristics of Christ.

> *"There is therefore now no condemnation to them which are in Christ Jesus, who walk not after the flesh, but after the Spirit."*
>
> — ROMANS 8:1 KJV

According to the Oxford Language, accusation means "a charge or claim that someone has something illegal or wrong." And that is what the enemy does– accuses. The enemy reminds us of what we have done, but God comes to forgive. The enemy comes day and night to accuse, while God comes to save those who are lost. An accusation is a charge, indictment, and bondage, while freedom is a release and pardon. The Lord gave us a way to escape accusations of the enemy. And if we're not careful, we will do what the enemy does— remind others of what they have done!

Most of the time, unforgiveness occurs when a person is hurt by another. Actions of another can cause a person deep emotional pain. As humans, we have faults and are prone to hurting a person, either intentionally or unintentionally. So, to ask for forgiveness, we must acknowledge and admit what we have done. To repent means that you never want to do that certain action again. The Holy Spirit can help us if we truly want help.

> *"But He [Jesus] was wounded for our transgres-*
> *sions, He was bruised for our iniquities: the*

chastisement of our peace was upon Him; and
with His stripes we are healed."

— ISAIAH 53:5 KJV

God shows us in His Word that He was wounded by our sins. The Lord can heal our emotions as well as our physical bodies. Forgiveness from the Lord is continual. Honestly, I have had to ask the Lord for forgiveness daily. We want the Lord to forgive us each time we ask, but at times, we are not so forgiving of others. We need mercy, and we must give mercy. How can we not show mercy when the Lord has been so merciful to us?

THE KING & THE SERVANT

Let's consider the case in Scripture of the man who was forgiven much, but was unable to forgive little.

> *"Then came Peter to him, and said, Lord, how often*
> *shall my brother sin against me, and I forgive*
> *him? till seven times?*
> *Jesus saith unto him, I say not unto thee, Until*
> *seven times: but, Until seventy times seven.*
> *Therefore is the kingdom of heaven likened unto a*
> *certain king, which would take account of his*
> *servants.*
> *And when he had begun to reckon, one was brought*
> *unto him, which owed him ten thousand*
> *talents.*
> *But forasmuch as he had not to pay, his lord*
> *commanded him to be sold, and his wife, and*

*children, and all that he had, and payment to
be made.*
*The servant therefore fell down, and worshipped
him, saying, Lord, have patience with me, and I
will pay thee all.*
*Then the lord of that servant was moved with
compassion, and loosed him, and forgave him
the debt.*
*But the same servant went out, and found one of his
fellowservants, which owed him an hundred
pence: and he laid hands on him, and took him
by the throat, saying, Pay me that thou owest.*
*And his fellowservant fell down at his feet, and
besought him, saying, Have patience with me,
and I will pay thee all."*

— MATTHEW 18:21-29 KJV

The servant was humble when he needed forgiveness; he begged, pleaded, and fell down before his lord. However, when it was his turn to show forgiveness and mercy, he showed none. Have you ever begged the Lord for forgiveness, and He forgave you, but when it was your turn to forgive, you showed the person no mercy? This ought not to be; grace and mercy is what the Lord shows to us, and we should ask Him to help us to do the same for others.

According to Bible.com, grace means, "generous, free and totally unexpected and underserved." We did not deserve forgiveness, but the Lord is faithful and forgiving.

SHERITA C. WHITE

"But if ye forgive not men their trespasses, neither will your Father forgive your trespasses."

— MATTHEW 6:15 KJV

The Lord is telling us that if we don't forgive, we should not expect Him to forgive our wrongdoings. We have no right to be unforgiving when God forgives us many times.

I personally have regretted some of my former actions and decisions. Regret has taught me mercy. When a person sincerely repents to the Lord, and to anyone involved, the ability to apologize is a privilege, regardless of whether the other person accepts it. But there is a balance here...at one point, I was just apologizing over and over again and again to the point of begging for forgiveness. I asked for forgiveness for all my past mistakes, feeling guilty and ashamed.

One day, the Lord told me to stop apologizing and that I was "off the hook." Our sins are covered by the Blood of Jesus. However, some people will never let you off the hook. It is very heartbreaking to experience someone bringing back up your old mistakes after you have repented and apologized to that person.

If you feel like you cannot forgive, remember how often we have to go to the Lord for forgiveness, daily. Remembering this should help us to be more forgiving and merciful. In her book, "The Power of Forgiveness," Marilyn Hickey wrote: "Forgiveness is not a feeling. You have to forgive by faith." Sometimes it takes time to forgive, but if we are like our Father, we can forgive instantly. It's dangerous not to forgive instantly, because it can grow into bitterness.

Accusations, unforgiveness, and bitterness are like being in prison for both the one who is seeking forgiveness and the one who will not forgive. The reason we often find it hard to forgive

96

is that we feel like we are to be owed something. We're looking for an apology that we may never get, but you can feel confident that you obeyed the Lord and seek forgiveness. Jesus paid the ultimate price for us. Jesus was the best example of forgiveness.

> *"Then said Jesus, Father, forgive them; for they know not what they do. And they parted his raiment, and cast lots."*
>
> — LUKE 23:34 KJV

So when that person comes back to ask for forgiveness, that means God is working on them. The Lord may have opened their eyes to see what they have done, even if it's days or years later. Some people are truly penitent for the things they have done. God even knows about secret sins, and He will forgive you because unforgiveness can eat away at you. The Holy Spirit would not let me have peace, even though I had repented to the Lord.

> *"He that covereth his sins shall not prosper: but whoso confesseth and forsaketh them shall have mercy."*
>
> — PROVERBS 28:13 KJV

According to Oxford Language, penitent means, "feeling or showing sorrow and regret for having done wrong." The one who is seeking forgiveness is pledging to be released from the wrong they have done, and they put themselves in a cell to be reminded of what they have done.

"A brother offended is harder to be won than a
strong city: and their contentions are like the
bars of a castle."

— PROVERBS 18:19 KJV

According to the Oxford Language, fortified means "provided with defensive works as protection against attack." Only
God can touch someone who is defensive and protective. Once
you have asked for forgiveness, you then have to forgive yourself. When you've done all that you can do, all you can do is
just stand. Ask the Lord for help.

"Brethren, if a man be overtaken in a fault, ye
which are spiritual, restore such an one in the
spirit of meekness; considering thyself, lest thou
also be tempted."

— GALATIANS 6:1 KJV

It is so tempting to reveal someone's faults and condemn
them for what they have done. Most of us forget about our
own sins, but we can easily point out the sins of others. It's
amazing to me how religious people can be some of the most
critical and judgmental people, as if we have never done
anything wrong in our entire lives. Thank you, God, for
redemption!

"Being justified freely by his grace through the
redemption that is in Christ Jesus."

— ROMANS 3:24 KJV

*"Ask, and it shall be given you; seek, and ye shall
find; knock, and it shall be opened unto you."*

— MATTHEW 7:7 KJV

THE WOMAN WHO COMMITTED ADULTERY VS DAVID'S AFFAIR WITH BATHSHEBA

It comes back to how we judge people with words. Let's look at the woman in the Bible who committed adultery.

Jesus went unto the mount of Olives.
And early in the morning he came again into the
temple, and all the people came unto him; and
he sat down, and taught them.
And the scribes and Pharisees brought unto him a
woman taken in adultery; and when they had
set her in the midst,
They say unto him, Master, this woman was taken
in adultery, in the very act.
Now Moses in the law commanded us, that such
should be stoned: but what sayest thou?
This they said, tempting him, that they might have
to accuse him. But Jesus stooped down, and
with his finger wrote on the ground, as though
he heard them not.
So when they continued asking him, he lifted up
himself, and said unto them, He that is without
sin among you, let him first cast a stone at her.
And again he stooped down, and wrote on the
ground.
And they which heard it, being convicted by their
own conscience, went out one by one, beginning

*at the eldest, even unto the last: and Jesus was
left alone, and the woman standing in the
midst.*

*When Jesus had lifted up himself, and saw none but
the woman, he said unto her, Woman, where
are those thine accusers? hath no man
condemned thee?*

*She said, No man, Lord. And Jesus said unto her,
Neither do I condemn thee: go, and sin no more.*

— JOHN 8:1-11 KJV

First of all, Let's look at the words they spoke and how they accused the woman caught in adultery. It was the people who forgot about their own sins. It was religious people— the scribes and Pharisees; they brought her and set her in the midst. They put her right where everyone could see her. The woman did not commit adultery alone, yet the man was never mentioned. Her accusers went on to say: "Let's kill her. Let's stone her death." We must not be so quick to judge others because there are always two sides to the story. A religious spirit is so damaging; it condemns and points fingers at others, forgetting that we have all sinned and come short of the glory of God (Romans 3:23).

*"For all have sinned, and come short of the glory of
God."*

— ROMANS 3:23 KJV

- Why did she do this?
- Was she looking for love in men?
- Was she hurting?

- Was she angry about the way someone treated her?
- Was it just lust?
- Was she broken by words?
- Was it generational, based on something that she saw in her own family?

We may never know all the details about what happened. No matter what their actions or intentions were, God saw her. He loved and redeemed her. Sin is never justified; however, we still must not judge. A person's life can change if they are willing to change. They just have to ask the Lord to help them.

After this incident, we don't hear anything further about this woman. It is my belief that this woman's life has completely changed. Her name was never mentioned again, although she was known by what she did, her new identity was completely made possible by Christ's presence and power working in her life..

Let's explore King David who was identified as a man after God's own heart, yet David committed the same sin of adultery (2 Samuel 11:1, 12:9). This is how we can label others by what they did. But was David any better than the women we just mentioned because he was a king? Was his sin of adultery a lesser offense because she was caught in the very act? We know that David deliberately planned his sinful act. What both stories have in common is that the Lord forgave them both. The Lord forgives from the least of these to the greatest, and He never gives up on any of us.

If we're not careful, we may do the same thing. We may judge a person, condemn them, and forget the things the Lord has forgiven us from. How does this relate to words? The scribes and Pharisees accused the woman with their words. People will accuse you of things you didn't even do. And if you did do it, there is nothing much you can do about your past sins. The only thing you can do is repent to God and the person you did wrong towards, forgive yourself, and move forward.

Forgiving yourself requires you to go to the Lord and say: "Lord, the truth is I did speak wrong, and I did do wrong, but I ask for your help to let it go." Also, it requires you to go to the person and ask for forgiveness. I have seen people take pleasure in always reminding others what they have done to them. You can ask them for forgiveness a million times, and they will still bring it up. That's when you know there is malice. Even when it comes to ourselves, I remember how I kept asking for forgiveness. Then, the Lord said, "Forgive yourself." We have to learn to forgive ourselves at some point after you have apologized and repented. You can't keep reminding yourself of what you have done after you have attempted with a sincere heart to seek forgiveness.

According to the Oxford Language, malice is the "intention or desire to do evil" or "ill will." When a person hates someone and wants to seek revenge, they desire to inflict injury, harm, or suffering on another– it's a deep-seated meanness. Synonyms for malice are spitefulness, spite, hatred, hate, bitterness, evil intentions, and revenge.

> *"He [God] will turn again, he will have compassion upon us; he will subdue our iniquities; and thou wilt cast all their sins into the depths of the sea."*
>
> — MICAH 7:19 KJV

I'm so glad we have a heavenly Father who forgives our sins and even forgets our sins when others don't. Lord, help us to forgive often and instantly like You do!

THE STORY OF JOB

> *"A friend loveth at all times, and a brother is born*
> *for adversity."*

> — PROVERBS 17:17 KJV

Friendships are very important in life; they can develop into either intimacy or a surface friendship. Did you know friendships are very important to the Lord? The Lord said that He sticks closer to us than a brother (Proverbs 18:24). Jesus is a faithful friend; His friendship is never based on what we do or do not do.

> *"He that sweareth to his own hurt, and changeth*
> *not."*

> — PSALM 15:4 KJV

Even if you change your mind, it doesn't mean you aren't a sincere friend. One-sided friendships are not fun; they are actually very hurtful, especially when your intentions are good.

Let's look at Job's friends in the Bible. In Job 4-23, Job's friends were initially supportive, but then they started talking about him. I can clearly understand why it's just better to be quiet. While being quiet can sometimes be difficult, it's better in the long run.

> *"There's a time to keep silent, and a time to speak."*

> — ECCLESIASTES 3:7 KJV

Job was dealing with some struggles and losses. So, Job's friends began to accuse him of doing evil and abandoning God. According to Job's friends, Job must have done something wrong for him to be experiencing these things. If you tell your friends your problems, and they start accusing you, and fault-finding, then those may be the wrong type of friends.

Life's circumstances can show you who your real friends are. Some people are not equipped to deal with your issues (or vice versa), but some have an anointing to pray you through. Again, we must be careful who we confide in. Some may not tell other people, but they will continue to remind you of what you told them. This makes a person wish they had never told that person in the first place. Therefore, it's important that we ask God to help us to be a true friend like how He is to us!

PERSONAL REFLECTION

Have you ever wrongly accused someone? Has someone ever wrongly accused you? Did forgiveness take place afterward? I challenge you to ask God to help you forgive someone who has hurt you deeply.

_____
_____
_____
_____
_____
_____
_____
_____
_____
_____
_____
_____
_____
_____
_____
_____
_____
_____
_____
_____
_____
_____
_____
_____
_____

SHERITA C. WHITE

HEALING THROUGH GOD'S WORD

WORDS & THE HEART

The words we speak and the condition of our heart are interconnected; they go hand-and-hand.

"O generation of vipers, how can ye, being evil, speak good things? for out of the abundance of the heart the mouth speaketh."

— MATTHEW 12:34 KJV

What is in a person's heart will usually come out through a person's mouth. A person can only hide it for so long. The Lord reveals His heart to us through the Word of God. In the Bible, the heart is considered the seat of life, soul, spirit, and strength. Hence, it means mind, soul, spirit, or one's entire emotional nature and understanding. The heart is the organ that is said to have the ability to reason, question, meditate, motivate, and think.

*"Keep thy heart with all diligence; for out of it are
the issues of life."*

— PROVERBS 4:23 KJV

Life is in your heart, because your heart controls what you think, say, and do. By allowing only godly, loving, confident, and helpful things into your heart, you will become more godly, loving, and mature. We must hide God's Word in our hearts. A person can speak words to break a person's heart. How is it possible that words can break a person's heart? This is because words have life-giving or life-destroying power. Only God can see in the spirit realm how a spoken word affects a person. Therefore, we must think before we speak. Words can damage and destroy marriages. Words have initiated wars. But the good news is, words can heal and bring deliverance.

Sometimes, we should be mindful of keeping certain matters of the heart to ourselves. We should consider: "Do I really need to say this? Will this hurt someone, if I say this?" However, there are some people who speak out of anger or malicious intent without regard for the consequences. But those who know the seriousness and the impact of their words, do care. The Bible says that we will give an account. So, before we say something, we should pray and say, "Lord, guard my heart and my tongue today! Watch over what I think and say today!"

*"But I say unto you, That every idle word that men
shall speak, they shall give account thereof in
the day of judgment."*

— MATTHEW 12:36 KJV

Most of the time, we point out the obvious of what most people consider to be classified as big sins: cursing, fornication, adultery, and drinking. The sins we may forget about are the sins we commit by the words we speak. God records what we say, and we must give an account. I asked the Lord, "Isn't that harsh, like every empty word? Lord, why will every empty word be counted in judgment?" We all may have at some point said something that was unpleasant. I asked God, "Lord, does all of that count?" And He replied, "Words have the ability to create a feeling or a reaction."

I once worked for a company that provided a list of words for staff to use when talking to customers. The list contained words such as: "perfect" and "wonderful," and keywords to avoid such as: "unfortunate" and "be patient." Instead of saying, "I don't know," we had to say, "Allow me to find the answer." So, that's why it is best for us to examine ourselves and take inventory of every empty and idle word because it creates a certain atmosphere. Even if the person doesn't hear it, God hears it. By speaking out into the atmosphere, we are either creating a world around us that is either peaceful or chaotic. Words are creative! God created the world with His Words. So, we must be careful not to use our words maliciously.

Evil, demonic words (such as name-calling) that attack a person's character with the intent to harm, with no regard for that person's feelings, hurt the heart of God. He does not want us to allow evil words to come out of our mouths.

> *"For he that will love life, and see good days, let him refrain his tongue from evil, and his lips that they speak no guile."*
>
> — 1 PETER 3:10 KJV

"Wherefore laying aside all malice, and all guile, and hypocrisies, and envies, and all evil speakings."

— 1 PETER 2:1 KJV

For instance, when you have shared something personal or confessed a sin to someone, that individual out of anger, may start reminding you of your faults, or use your personal information against you, saying, "Remember, when...?"

Now, here's a true story that happened in my life. I trusted and confided in one of my dearest friends because she was a praying woman of God, and I liked what she would always say. When we would pray or talk about a subject matter, my dearest friend Sister Vera Taylor would say, "I am going to ask the Lord to erase it from my mind." There were literally times I would ask her if she remembered what I had said, and she would say that she had forgotten. This was because she understood the importance of what it meant to be free from something once it was released to God.

The Word of God cleanses us, and His Word is His heart. The way He speaks in the Bible reveals how He feels about us. The Word of God is correct and shows us God's everlasting love toward us. If someone does us wrong, we must show mercy, just as God shows mercy towards us. We are all humans, and sometimes we will do hurtful things.

"For all have sinned, and come short of the glory of God."

— ROMANS 3:23 KJV

We are born sinners and are not perfect like God. However,

we should strive to be Christ-like and have compassion for others, through the things we say and do. If someone does care about us, that person will cease the harmful communication, and their actions toward us will change for the better. Let's look at how our Lord's heart is towards us.

> *"And above all things have fervent charity among*
> *yourselves: for charity shall cover the multitude*
> *of sins."*

> — I PETER 4:8 KJV

If we cannot have charity, then this is a heart and love issue. Thus, we must ask the Lord to create in us a clean heart, so that we are able to cover others in a spirit of love. Some people just cannot hold their tongue, they have to say what they think, as they feel that it just has to be said. On the other hand, some people will ponder before speaking, to consider how what they have to say will affect others.

> *"And the tongue is a fire, a world of iniquity: so is*
> *the tongue among our members, that it defileth*
> *the whole body, and setteth on fire the course of*
> *nature; and it is set on fire of hell."*

> — JAMES 3:6 KJV

Now that we are aware of this, our daily prayer should be, "Lord, guard my thoughts and my tongue every day."

> *"Wherefore, my beloved brethren, let every man be
> swift to hear, slow to speak, slow to wrath."*

— JAMES 1:19 KJV

Based upon this verse, we should also pray to Him saying,
"Lord, help me to listen more than I speak."

> *"I sought the Lord, and he heard me, and delivered
> me from all my fears.
> They looked unto him, and were lightened: and
> their faces were not ashamed.
> This poor man cried, and the Lord heard him, and
> saved him out of all his troubles.
> The angel of the Lord encampeth round about them
> that fear him, and delivereth them.
> O taste and see that the Lord is good: blessed is the
> man that trusteth in him."*

— PSALM 34:4-8 KJV

We should come to the Lord with our thoughts and feelings because the Holy Spirit is our Comforter. We should look
to Him for guidance before we do or say anything; we should
strive to be Christ-like in our thoughts and actions, and go to
Him for instruction.

> *"For who hath known the mind of the Lord, that he
> may instruct him? But we have the mind of
> Christ."*

— 1 CORINTHIANS 2:16 KJV

FROM BROKEN TO HEALED

> *"He sent his word, and healed them, and deliv-*
> *ered them from their destructions."*

> — PSALM 107:20

To heal, you must remove yourself from an environment that is intended to destroy you. You must not allow a person to continually speak hurtful words over your spirit man.

> *"You cannot heal in the environment you were*
> *hurt in."*

> — ANONYMOUS

World-renowned physicist Albert Einstein once said, "Insanity is doing the same thing over and over and expecting different results." It is with intentionality that I am being careful about how I am writing this book because it is my belief that words can affect a person's soul and spirit. While we cannot always physically see how words affect a person with the naked eye, it's like the imagery of an arrow piercing through the heart.

> *"So when they continued asking him, he lifted up*
> *himself, and said unto them, He that is without*
> *sin among you, let him first cast a stone at her."*

> — JOHN 8:7 KJV

This Scripture further explains just how words can be very powerful. While people may not throw stones in terms of a physical object, they can throw stones with their words.

> *"Thou givest thy mouth to evil, and thy tongue frameth deceit. Thou sittest and speakest against thy brother; thou slanderest thine own mother's son."*
>
> — PSALM 50:19-20 KJV

> *"For it was You who created my inward parts; you knit me together in my mother's womb. I will praise You because I have been fearfully and wonderfully made."*
>
> — PSALM 139:13 KJV

It doesn't matter if you have a problem or not, you mean something to God. In light of this, it is important to be cautious when using social media and listening to others since they can rob you of hope, if you let them. You must know God for yourself and believe what He says about you, even if you have an imperfection, which we all do.

It is interesting to look at the women of the Bible because they are relatable. In the Body of Christ, the woman with the issue of blood is mentioned often. Let's take a closer look at her story.

> *"Now there was a woman who had been suffering from hemorrhages for twelve years: and though she had spent all she had on physicians, no on could cure her. She came up behind Jesus and*

touched the fringe oh his clothes, immediately
her hemorrhage stopped."

— LUKE 8:43-48 KJV

The one thing we observe is that she was determined to receive her healing. She was desperate and at a low point in her life. Although this woman was afflicted with an issue of blood, she was an example for others with problems like hers. She wanted to be whole again. Physically and financially, she was at the end of her rope. Because of her condition, she was shunned. It's no doubt that she was talked about. She was probably looked at in a funny way. But in spite of everything she did to be clean, she could not change her condition. She spent everything she had to be healed. She didn't have a husband, children, or friends. Nothing she tried worked.

At this time, this woman was condemned by religious law. She was condemned to believe that she was soiled, unworthy, and unclean. She was also told that anything she touched would be unclean. So, it became her responsibility not to contaminate others because of her condition. She was seen as an outcast and no longer valuable to society. So, she had to step outside of the environment that condemned her in order to reach Jesus and get her healing. In our society, condemnation is quite common. We are definitely living in the last days. The world has truly become cold and heartless, anytime a person can use social media as a means to speak negatively about a person's value and worth. The Bible speaks about the love of many growing cold.

"And because iniquity shall abound, the love of many shall wax cold."

— MATTHEW 24:1 KJV

There was no mention of this woman's age, size, finances, or marital status. The focus was on her condition and need for healing. Her healing was immediate when she sought help from Jesus the Healer. When we acknowledge our issues, we can receive help. Our issues may be anger, bitterness, unforgiveness, alcoholism, drugs, etc. We can be healed by God regardless of our condition.

"For I am the Lord: I will speak and the words that I shall speak shall come to pass, it shall be no more prolonged, for in your day, O rebellious house, will I say the word and will perform it said the Lord."

— EZEKIEL 12:25 KJV

Many of us have experienced challenges in our lives. Our challenges may have been financial, physical, emotional, familial, or interpersonal. Regardless of the type of problem, we must be like this woman. Her first step was acknowledging that she had a problem; then, she tried using her resources to solve the issue. Eventually, she ran out of resources and could not fix her condition. She knew that Jesus could bring resolve to her problem. If she touched the hem of His garment, she would be healed. Your healing may not always be instantaneous like the woman with the issue of blood, but God will bring healing according to His will for you. You will receive healing through the power of God's Word.

Healing comes through discovering your identity. We don't have to accept negative labeling and hurtful things people pronounce on us. To help us identify and reject unhealthy labeling, it's important to know your identity in Christ through His Word. We are not depressed, rejected, addicted, or anything else contrary to God's Word. Whatever your specific situation may be, identify it and speak against those lies of the enemy through prayer and God's Word.

The process of healing occurs both naturally and spiritually. My spiritual father, Bishop Daniel M. Jordan, taught me that God can heal instantaneously or gradually in the process. As far as matters of the heart are concerned, it's always a rule of thumb to treat others as you want to be treated. We all need grace. When a person needs grace, it may cause them to be more humble. It'll enable them to empathize with others who have also made mistakes.

No matter what type of abuse a person has experienced in their life, the only solution is prayer and God's Word. You can reverse the impact of the words that hurt you by praying God's Word over your life. And although it may be a fight or a struggle to overcome, it is possible through God's Word. There will always be something you or someone else said to you that the enemy will try to remind you of, but you have to learn how to reject every negative thought and word that comes to steal your joy.

Just like Job, we all have gone through challenging circumstances. Job was an upright man; he dealt with various types of calamities and losses. He was a good man, and the Lord tested him. Through Job's story, we learn that some things come to make us strong, whereas other things come to allow us to have compassion for others. Remember: Words are the God-given power that we have right here on the earth. My prayer is that the Lord continues to help us to use our words to bless someone's life.

PERSONAL REFLECTION

Have you ever been given a label that attacked your identity? Today, I challenge you to rebuke this label and write down who God says you are.

_____

_____

_____

_____

_____

_____

_____

_____

_____

_____

_____

_____

_____

_____

_____

_____

_____

_____

_____

_____

_____

_____

_____

_____

_____

_____

_____

_____

_____

_____

SHERITA C. WHITE

PRAYERS &
ENCOURAGEMENT

*Rejoice in hope, be patient in tribulation, be
constant in prayer.*

— ROMANS 12:12

PRAYER TO DESTROY NEGATIVE WORDS

Lord Jesus, I (we) ask you to destroy all ill-spoken words, ill
wishes, and every idle word spoken contrary to God's original
plans and purposes. Your Word says, "Your tongue devises
wickedness; it is like a sharp razor, working deceitfully" (Psalm
52:2 KJV). Lord Jesus, I (we) ask that You destroy the curses
associated with these utterances. You decree and declare that:
they shall not stand; they shall not come to pass; they shall not
take root; and their violent verbal dealings are returned to
them double-fold, according to Isaiah 54:17.

CONFESS THE WORD OVER YOUR LIFE

Do not depend on others for your spiritual well-being. Confess God's Word over your life, and route the enemy from your life with prayers to God. Do not allow self-pity or fear to hold you back. Stir yourself up to offer your prayers to God, for this is your key to victory. Follow the example of the apostle Paul. When the enemy bound him with chains and cast him in prison, he was encouraged to speak God's Word more courageously and fearlessly than before. When the enemy tries to discourage you and to defeat you, boldly speak God's Word to him.

PRAYER FOR DELIVERANCE

Father, I will experience deliverance and release from the power of Satan, as I boldly confess Your Word over my life. My mouth will speak words of wisdom, and the utterance of my heart will give understanding. Touch my lips with Your Spirit, as you did for Isaiah and Daniel of old, and I will speak the truth of Your Word, continually.

———

*The prayers and encouragement included above have been quoted from the Red Prayer Book from Christian Word Ministries.**

ACKNOWLEDGMENTS

This book would not be possible with the love and support of many!

First, I want to extend a special thank you to my Lord and Savior Jesus Christ, who has helped guide me through life's journeys. He is my best friend and has never left my side, no matter what. Thank you for loving me and for always being there for me through thick and thin!

I want to extend a special thank you to my mother, Cheryeal C. Mack. Mom, the older I get, the more I need you. I can always talk to you about life and situations. You always make the most sense, even when I don't want to hear it. I can always hear your voice saying certain things, and it makes me so glad that you've been there for me. I appreciate you for saying, "Who told you that?" or "Where did you get that from?" You always asked, "Did God tell you that?" You always lead me back to the Word of God. I love you very much and appreciate you more than I can say. I love you, always!

I want to say thank you to my spiritual father in the Gospel, Bishop Daniel M. Jordan of the Pentecostal Church of God in Christ (Kansas City) who taught me so many things about the Lord.

I want to thank Evangelist Leigh Drew (who made my ideas into artwork), and *many other teachers of the Gospel of Jesus Christ.*

I want to say thank you to Mr. & Mrs. James C. White.

Thank you to Bishop Stan Gleason, Pastor Justin Gleason, and *Pastor Gary Morgan* of The Life Church Kansas City for the Word of God, prayers, and encouragement.

Thank you to my dearest friend #1 Spot, Sister Vera Taylor.

Thank you, also, to my dearest friend Sister Janet Williams.

A special thank you to Evangelist Valorie McCall at Sarah Prays. Thank you for all of your prayers.

I am also thankful for my family and friends, especially my twin sister Selita C. Johnson, who stood by me through some of life's toughest situations and circumstances.

I am thankful to my friends who told me to just write! I am thankful for all of your support and wisdom.

Last, but not least, I also want to say thank you to Nicole Queen and Vision Publishing House, who always encouraged me with my writing— every step of the way.

ABOUT THE AUTHOR

 Sherita C. White is a servant who experienced the call of the Lord in her life at an early age. This call was later confirmed by her spiritual father in the Gospel, Bishop Daniel M. Jordan of the Pentecostal Church of God in Christ, located Kansas City, Missouri. On September 9, 1994, Bishop Jordan prophesied that the Lord would call her to be a missionary.

Years later, she was recommended to receive her missionary license; she obtained her license through the Pentecostal Church of God in Christ. The Lord used her to bring services together to bless the Body of Christ. Sherita has done services, titled "Lord Show Me Your Glory," and "What About The Children." Her first revival was entitled "Purge Me Lord." She also spoke at women's conferences, prayer breakfasts, and Encounters.

Missionary White knows that the Bible is like no other book on the face of the earth. She understands that it's God speaking, Himself, who manifests change in our lives for healing and guidance. This caused Sister White to start a ministry entitled "Study The Word Ministry." Sister White has a passion for women who are hurting. It is her prayer to guide women to a place of deliverance, healing, and peace through God's Word, transitioning them from brokenness to healing.

Currently, Sister White resides in Lee Summit with her daughter Promise White.

T-SHIRTS

JESUS LET ME OFF THE HOOK   **PRAY IT BEFORE YOU SAY IT!**

AVAILABLE SIZES: S, M, L, XL

UNISEX SIZES AVAILABLE

AVAILABLE COLORS: GRAY, PURPLE, LILAC, WHITE

PRICE: $25 (S, M, L) | $30 (XL)

ORDER FORM

NAME:

ADDRESS:

PHONE NUMBER:

T-SHIRT SIZE:

T-SHIRT COLOR:

SUBMIT YOUR ORDER TO:
STUDYTHEWORDMINISTRIES2021@YAHOO.COM

SUBMIT PAYMENT:
PAYPAL: SWHITE1212863

FOR ADDITIONAL INFORMATION, PLEASE CALL:
(816) 272 - 5077

www.ingramcontent.com/pod-product-compliance
Lightning Source LLC
Chambersburg PA
CBHW071003120626
46546CB00003B/912